On My Way to Where

ON MY WAY TO WHERE

Dory Previn

The McCall Publishing Company
New York

*Published simultaneously in Canada by
Doubleday Canada Ltd., Toronto*

*Library of Congress Catalog Card Number: 76–160057
ISBN 0–8415–0120–3*

*The McCall Publishing Company
230 Park Avenue, New York, N.Y. 10017*

PRINTED IN THE UNITED STATES OF AMERICA

Design by Tere LoPrete

for my friend
nikolas venet
who taught me
to appreciate
one-note creatures

Contents

On My Way to Where

on my way to where

the thought
he'll leave
bitterly burns
and my despondence
grows
i lost my blue buttons
he sent me
blue buttons
on my birthday
but my blue buttons
came loose
loose

loose
lucy brown
lucy in the sky
luce
lucent
lucid
lucidity
lucifer
light
hang luce
stay loose

i
how did i get this way
i was
what was i going to say
i was on
how did i get in here
i was on my
wasn't i here last year
i was on my way
why have they locked me in
i was on my way to
who is my next of kin
christ
won't i ever win
i paid

my airplane fare
i was
on my way to where. . . .

I

i exist

i ain't his child

my daddy says
i ain't his child
ain't that something
ain't that wild
daddy says
i ain't his child
ain't that something
wild

my hair is curly
my freckles are tan
could my daddy be

the garbage man
my legs are stumpy
my fingers are short
like my uncle will
who is the
bowling sport
my eyes are slanty
like mister woo
hey
mister laundryman
is it you
i'm ugly as steve
with the big mustache
but mama says poles
are a piece of trash

my daddy says
i ain't his child
ain't that something
ain't that wild
daddy says
i ain't his child
ain't that something
wild

hey
anybody i might
have missed

would you care to state
that i exist
i ain't quite sure
what it is
i did
to make him swear
that i ain't
his kid
but he told mama
and she told me
back when i was
just about three
she felt my face
and she
kind of smiled
and she said
he says
you ain't his child

my daddy says
i ain't his child
ain't that something
ain't that wild
daddy says
i ain't his child
ain't that
something
wild

with my daddy in the attic

with my
daddy in the attic
with my
daddy in the attic
that is where
my being wants to bed

with the mattress ticking showing
and the tattered pillow slip
and the pine
unpainted rafters overhead

12

with the
door closed on my mama
and my sibling competition
and my shirley temple doll
that truly cries
and my essay on religion
with the pasted paper star
proving tangibly
i'd won the second prize

with my daddy in the attic
with my daddy in the attic
that is where
my dark attraction lies
with his madness on the nightstand
placed beside
his loaded gun
in the terrifying nearness
of his eyes

with no
window spying neighbors
and no
husbands in the future
to intrude
upon our attic
past the stair
where we'll live on

peanut butter
spread across assorted crackers
and he'll play
his clarinet
when i despair.

aunt rose and the blessed event

daddy boarded up
the dining room
and locked us in
we three
four and a half months
we lived in that room
my mama the baby and me
my mama slept on the table
i slept on a cot
the baby was in a basket
i hated it a lot

we'd listen
till he went off to work
then we'd sneak out
for eggs
i'd run around the kitchen
to stretch my stumpy legs
we'd finish our eggs and coffee
then we'd make it neat
so daddy wouldn't go all crazy
'cause we came out to eat

one monday
after christmas day
he let my mama free
the week after that
i came out
the baby
he still wouldn't see
at night we'd go back in there
the reason i forgot
the baby didn't know the diff'rence
i hated it a lot

aunt rose came by
to visit us
bring out the kid
she said
mama says

godinhisgoodnessno
that man would shoot me dead
my mama says
he ain't seen it yet
her face went white as pearl
he don't know if the kid i had
is a boy or a little girl

well
aunt rose brought out
the baby
and laid it in the light of the tree
daddy arrived home
early from the job
and pretended
like he didn't see

so rosie picked up
the baby
and shoved it at him
on the spot
i watched him
take my sister
i hated it a lot

from then on
we were a family
we even had some fun

the boards
on the dining room door
came down
and daddy put away his gun
and
i forgot it happened
like something
i'd been dreaming
till eighteen odd years later
when i suddenly woke up
screaming.

esther's first communion

when she made her first communion
esther made the perfect union
in her dress of white and wispy veil
esther's parents said to please us
you got to go and marry jesus
and her father took her to the altar rail

when she made her first communion
esther made the perfect union
and that night she thought of him in bed
she decided if he sees us

19

we ought to get a look at jesus
and she began to see the one she wed

i began to see little jesus
he was sitting on my bed
that's what esther told her mother
and to which her mother said
you're an evil child to tease us
glory be i hope to jesus
that your father never hears this
he would wash your mouth with soap

when she made her first communion
esther made the perfect union
but she never saw his face again
yeah her mother said don't tease us
so instead of seeing jesus
she began to see a lot of other men

what she saw was quite a collection
older men and young ones too
cousins friends and even a brother
one at a time or quite a few
she began to see a gay uncle
who resembled billy graham
she began to see perfect strangers
she didn't even know by name

when she made her first communion
esther made the perfect union
but she never saw his face again
yeah her mother said don't tease us
so instead of seeing jesus
she began to see a lot of other men
but she never told her mother again
no she never told her mother again.

so long mom
so long dad

so long mom
so long dad
i just got married
but don't feel bad
you won't have to tell me
'bout the birds and bees
'cause for quite a few years
i've done as i please
and we're going out
to los angeles
where the oranges
grow on trees

22

i hate to fly
in an aeroplane
so we're gonna take
the choo-choo train
the endless trip
they say is worth
the chance to ball
in an upper berth

so long mom
so long dad
got something to tell you
but don't be mad
i married a guy
the two of you
used to describe as
a typical jew
i'm sorry
folks
he ain't our kind
but i don't think
jesus will mind

jesus' name was
emmanuel
he was a nice jewish boy
so what the hell
if he could stand it

well so can you
besides there's nothing
that you can do

so long mom
so long dad
i just got married
but don't feel bad
'cause we're going out
to los angeles
where the oranges
grow on trees
the oranges
grow on trees.

for my father

aftershock

the telephone rang
my sister calling
i got to run i said
nonononono
i just want
to tell you
to tell you
dad is dead
dad is dead?
well when did it happen?
six a.m.
said she
new york time

or california?
new york time
i see

the telephone rang
the week of the earthquake
death was still in the air
at six o one
the walls fell down
they never had a prayer
dad is dead?
well how is mother?
good as she
can be
say i said
when dad was goin'
did he happen
to ask
for me?

'member the way
i used to tap dance
lord it made him proud
he told his friends
(he never told me)
that i stood above the crowd
'member the way
he played the jew's harp

till he broke a tooth
why did he have
to turn against me
he loved me once
in his youth

but jesus
i couldn't live his life
make his fantasies real
i couldn't be him
i had to be me
i couldn't make up
for the deal
the dirty deal
he got in this world
he got in a
treacherous world
where six a.m.
suddenly breaks
with senseless death
and shocking quakes
senseless death
and shocking quakes
senseless death
and shocking quakes

the telephone rang
my sister calling

i'll go on fighting
his ghost
don't you know dad
the kid that hates
is the kid that loves
the most
dad is dead?
when did it happen?
six a.m.
said she
new york time
or california?
did he
ask
for me?

what did you say?
never mind
he died in his sleep

god is kind.

II /
i was you too long

lemon haired ladies

whatever you give me
i'll take as it comes
discarding self pity
i'll manage with crumbs
i'll settle for moments
i won't ask for life
i'll not expect labels
like lover or wife
if showing affection
embarrasses you
i will not depend

and i will not pursue
for you are
younger than i
younger than i
younger than i
and i am
wiser than you

the one a.m. phone calls
you're here then you're gone
come when you need me
i won't carry on
i'll simply accept you
the way that you are
unsure and unstructured
my door is ajar
those lemon haired ladies
of twenty or so
of course you must see them
just don't let me know
don't let me know
whatever you do
for you are
younger than i
younger than i
younger than i
and i am
weaker than you

i'll give you a year
maybe two
maybe three
then what will happen
where will i be
you'll still be a boy
but what about me
    what about me
    what about me

why must you treat me
with such little care
i've so much inside me
i'm aching to share
why am i constant
to someone like you
children don't know
the meaning of "true"
those lemon haired ladies
why must you see them
all that i want in your eyes
is to be them
time is on their side
that's all i lack
i wish you would just
go away
no
come back

come back
go away
come back
go away
what in hell can i do
i'm supposed to be wise
for i am
older than you
older than you

you
so self-centered
the games that you play
do as you please
you will anyway
of course you will see them
no use to pretend
for they are
younger than i
younger than i
those lemon haired ladies
and they will
win in the end.

men wander
women weep

men wander
women weep
women worry
while men are asleep
men wander
while women weep
and that's the way
it goes

i waited for you love
all last night
i listened to music
and kept on the light
i watched the morning

and walked the floor
till i heard your key
in my open door

men wander
women weep
women worry
while men are asleep
men wander
while women weep
and that's the way
it goes

as soon as i thought love
i heard your key
i put out the light love
so you wouldn't see
i shut off the music
and faced the wall
but it wasn't your key
i'd heard at all

men wander
women weep
women worry
while men are asleep
men wander
while women weep
and that's the way
it goes

tonight i am certain
i'll wait some more
till i hear your footstep
at my front door
if you don't show up love
i'll curse all men
and tomorrow night
i'll be waitin' again

men wander
women weep
women worry
while men are asleep
men wander
while women weep
and that's the way
it goes

love with women
is very deep
love with men
is a thing
that can keep
they won't admit it
but ev'ry woman knows
that's the way
it goes.

for five years
i was terrified
to get on a plane

i think i could have made it
but you killed me with conditions
just one suitcase
just one week
your own hotel

i can't meet you at the airport
i'll send someone out to get you
don't come monday
wait till tuesday
call me
swell

you can come to my rehearsals
but i'm busy on the weekend
i'll come any
way i love you
yes
but well

god i can't believe you're coming
i know isn't it fantastic
are you happy
wait till tuesday
go
to
hell.

i was you

i smiled
your smile
till my mouth
was set
and my face
was tight
and it wasn't right
it was wrong
i was you baby
i was you too long

i said
your words

till my throat
closed up
and i had
no voice
and i had
no choice
but to do your song
i was you baby
i was you too long

i lived
your life
till there was
no me
i was flesh
i was hair
but i wasn't there
it was wrong
i was you baby
i was you too long
and baby baby
the worst thing
to it
is that you let me
do it
so who was weak
and who was strong
for too long baby
i was you.

the new enzyme detergent
demise of ali macgraw

mine was a wednesday death
one afternoon
at approximately three-fifteen
soon after lunch
(we ate scrambled eggs together)
i gave up and died
nobody cried

friends were fooled
by the fact

i still breathed
and spoke
and smiled
and lied
in my handy dandy
imitation life disguise kit
i sent away for it
one box-top and a blue chip stamp
the styrofoam face
fits neatly
over the pre-recorded voice
and friends are deceived
nobody grieves

mine was a bloodless death
not grim not gory
more like ali macgraw's
new enzyme detergent demise
in "love story"
neat and tidy

unlike christ's on friday
mine was a wednesday death
one afternoon
at approximately three-fifteen
shortly before dinner
(i ate leftover meatloaf alone)

43

i was quietly laid to rest
nobody guessed

a handy disposable heart
beats time in a plastic breast
and so it goes
and nobody knows
i am
non
bio-degradable.

beware of young girls

beware
of young girls
who come to the door
wistful and pale
of twenty and four
delivering daisies
with delicate hands

beware
of young girls
too often they crave
to cry
at a wedding

and dance
on a grave

she was my friend
she was invited to my house
and though she knew
my love was true
and
no ordinary thing
she admired
my wedding ring
she admired my wedding ring

she was my friend
she sent us little silver gifts
oh what a rare
and happy pair
she
inevitably said
as she glanced
at my unmade bed
she admired
my unmade bed

she was my friend
i thought her motives were sincere
ah but this lass
it came to pass

had
a dark and different plan
she admired
my own sweet man
she admired
my own sweet man

we were friends
and she just took him from my life
so young and vain
she brought me pain
but
i'm wise enough to say
she will leave him
one thoughtless day
she'll just leave him
and go away

beware
of young girls
who come to the door
wistful and pale
of twenty and four
delivering daisies
with delicate hands

beware
of young girls

too often they crave
to cry
at a wedding
and dance
on a grave

beware of young girls
beware of young girls
beware

common sense, circa '35

why don't you leave him mama
how come you take it like that
boy mama if you had any sense
you'd walk out
and leave him flat

when i am big
no man will do
what daddy went
and did to you

i thought of this
that whole night long
how did mama
get so wrong?

common sense, circa '69

why don't you leave him dory
how come you take it like that
boy dory if you had any sense
you'd walk out
and leave him flat

but who's got sense
my mama cried
tucking me in
in 'thirty-five

now i am big
and recall that night
how did mama
get so right?

III /
a sadness in my head

twenty-mile zone

i was riding in my car
screaming at the night
screaming at the dark
screaming at fright
i wasn't doing nothing
just driving about
screaming at the dark
letting it out
that's all i was doing
just
letting it out

well along comes a motorcycle
very much to my surprise

i said officer was i speeding
i couldn't see his eyes
he said no you weren't speeding
and he felt where his gun was hung
he said lady you were screaming
at the top of your lung
and you were
doing it alone
you were doing it alone
you were screaming in your car
in a twenty-mile zone
you were doing it alone
you were doing it alone
you were screaming

i said i'll roll up all my windows
don't want to disturb the peace
i'm just a creature
who is looking
for a little release
i said
and what's so wrong with screaming
don't you do it at your games
when the quarterback
breaks an elbow
when the boxer beats and maims
but you were
doing it alone

you were doing it alone
you were screaming in your car
in a twenty-mile zone
you were doing it alone
you were doing it alone
you were screaming

i said animals roar
when they feel like
why can't we do that too
instead of screaming
banzai baby
in the war in the human zoo

he said i got to take you in now
follow me right behind
and let's have no more screaming
like you're out of your mind
so he climbed aboard his cycle
and his red-eyed headlight beamed
and his motor started spinning
and his siren screamed

he was doing it alone
he was doing it alone
he was screaming on his bike
in a twenty-mile zone
he was doing it alone

he was doing it alone
he was screaming
i was doing it alone
i was doing it alone
i was screaming in my car
in a twenty-mile zone
i was doing it alone
i was doing it alone
i was screaming
we were doing it together
we were doing it together
we were screaming at the dark
in a twenty-mile zone
we were doing it together
we were doing it together
we were screaming
we were doing it together
we were doing it
together
alone
in a twenty-mile zone.

mister whisper

when i am going
'round the bend
i got a wild
imaginary friend
when i am driven
up the wall
my old friend
he comes to call

mister whisper's
here again
mister whisper's
here again

he's back
in his apartment
in my head
he's back
in his apartment
like i said

just when life
can't get much worse
he tells me
reassuring things
says i'm the
center of the universe
says i'm as good as
presidents and kings

mister whisper's
here again
mister whisper's
here again
i think
i can control him
but instead
mister whisper
takes control
guides my heart
and rides my soul
the minute that

he steps
inside my head

just when i am
sure he'll stay
they shoot me
with a bolt or two
they try to drive
my mister friend
away
and damn it all
they nearly always do

mister whisper
don't go 'way
mister whisper
won't you stay
it gets so lonely
wish
that i were dead
listen whisper
please don't go
listen whisper
don't you know
i'd rather
madness
than this sadness
in my head

the thought
he'll leave
bitterly burns
and my despondence
grows
as soon as lonely
lonely sanity
returns
and old mister
old mister whisper
goes.

three-dollar room

why do i long
to take over the cross
what in the world
would be gained or be lost
why do i want
to replace sweet sufferin' jesus
who'd wake up and weep
the guests need their sleep

why do i feel
the need for to bleed
to do myself in

with this torturous deed
who down the hall
would be glad to be stuck
with the mess that remains
the desk clerk complains

why do i choose
to check out
unsuspected
some night in a
three-dollar room
no little white churches
were ever erected
for unwanted martyrs
(every three-dollar tomb
has color tv
included free)
nailed to the sheet
on a three-dollar bed
ain't no resurrectin'
the three-dollar dead
no refund allowed
for leaving too soon
says on the door
paid up till noon

yet i would dare
to bear my own blame

stealing from jesus
his sufferin' fame
why do i ask
to carry my luggage
pay my own bill
and leave when i will
some night in a
three-dollar room
let *me* atone
for nobody's sins
but my own.

two a.m. with a guard

it's two a.m.
i cannot sleep
i pace the halls
someone is calling
help me hey somebody help me
i guess it beats counting sheep
i know it beats counting sheep

it's two fifteen
i sit in fear
i have a guard
someone is sobbing

64

i love you yes no i don't
i guess the guard doesn't hear
i know the guard doesn't hear

it's three a.m.
someone just screamed
i stand aloof
and listen to the torment
jesus jesus jesus
i guess it's something someone dreamed
it must be something someone dreamed

i head for my room
well don't you see
i'd get some sleep
if they'd stop
calling cursing crying
if all those voices
would let me be
let me be
at two a.m.
when no one is awake
but me.

gotta stop depending

gotta stop depending
on those devils
gotta get my surface
neat and straight
why can't i just do it
lord i miss the trees
may i have a tranquilizer please?

gotta learn to face
the competition
everybody's scared
the same as me

wonder what they're thinking
something that i said
may i have two more to mend my head?

you sure i got no letter?
christ
these california showers
may i have a pill
to get some sleep?
all i need's a couple of hours
how come no one sends me flowers?

gotta stop pretending
i'm adjusted
screw them all
and let the surface crack
may i be psychotic?
please may i trip out?
may i be?
i mean
what i'm about?
may i?
may i?
may i?

visitor's hour

judy and don
came to see me
the technician undid the lock
i showed them
the inner attractions
the meds
the straps
the shock

nervously
don admitted
sensing danger of a kind

like someone might
hide in a doorway
and hit
him from
behind

i laughed
and reassured him
the techs are always on guard
one sign
of a patient's violence
they move in
hard

but
i had seen
a face in a doorway
i recalled when they had gone
a boy hid
behind don's shoulder
the boy
i'd seen
was don.

IV /
stay awhile and save my life

be my cover

lover lover
be my cover
till the night
begins to fade
oh the demons
i have danced with
lover lover
i'm afraid
to fall asleep
the night is dark and deep
and i am so afraid
to sleep

to fall asleep
and dream

lover lover
let your body
be my curtain
be my shade
i'm well acquainted
with confusion
lover lover
i'm afraid
to fall asleep
the night is dark and deep
and i am so afraid to sleep
to fall asleep
and dream

something waits
'neath the water
shapes and shadows
drifting near
someone watches
in the darkness
lover
won't you make them disappear
hold your tired girl
and kiss her
but don't you let her

close her eyes
god
i wish the reassuring sun
would rise

lover lover
be my cover
so those demons
won't parade
'round me
while i lie defenseless
lover lover
i'm afraid
to fall asleep
the night is dark and deep
and i am so afraid
to sleep
to fall asleep
and die.

yada yada la scala

yada yada yada yada yada
let's stop talking talking talking
wasting precious time
just a lot of empty noise
that isn't worth a dime
words of wonder
words of whether
should we shouldn't we
be together
yada yada yada yada yada

let's stop talking talking talking
taking up our lives

saying things that don't make sense
hoping help arrives
curse my questions
damn your qualms
tomorrow they could be
dropping bombs
and we go yada yada yada yada yada

so we sit
at a restaurant table
discussing reasons
we're unable to commit
that's not it
all i want
is to please and enjoy you
what makes you think
i'll be out to destroy you
if you commit
that's not it
is it something you sense
underneath my defenses
that makes me a threat
that's not it
and yet
suppose that's it?
ow wow wow
i don't want to
think about that now

let's stop talking talking talking
every lame excuse
justifying alibying
listen what's the use
the sparrow chirps
the chipmunk chatters
and we go on as mad as a hatter
and nothing at all gets said
talk to me please
in bed
where it matters
yada yada yada yada yada

the lady with the braid

would you care to stay till sunrise
it's completely your decision
it's just that going home is such a ride
going home is such a ride
going home is such a ride
going home is such a low and lonely ride

would you hang your denim jacket
near the poster by picasso
do you sleep on the left side or the right
would you mind if i leave on the light
would you mind if it isn't too bright

now i need the window open
so if you happen to get chilly
there's this coverlet my cousin hand crocheted
do you mind if the edges are frayed
would you like to unfasten my braid

shall i make you in the morning
a cup of instant coffee
i will sweeten it with honey and with cream
when you sleep
do you have dreams?
you can read the early paper
and i can watch you while you shave
oh god the mirror's cracked
when you leave
will you come back?
you don't have to answer that at all
the bathroom door is just across the hall
you'll find an extra towel on the rack
on the paisley patterned papered wall
there's a comb on the shelf
i papered that wall myself
that wall
myself

would you care to stay till sunrise
it's completely your decision
it's just the night cuts through me like a knife

would you care to stay awhile and save my life?
would you care to stay awhile and save my life?

i don't know what made me say that
i've got this funny sense of humor
you know i could not be downhearted if i tried
it's just that going home is such a ride
going home is such a ride
going home is such a ride
isn't going home a low and lonely ride?

angels and devils the following day

loved i two men
equally well
though they were diff'rent
as heaven and hell
one was an artist
one drove a truck
one would make love
the other would fuck
each treated me
the way he knew best
one held me lightly
one bruised my breast

and i responded
on two diff'rent levels
like children reacting
to angels and devils
one was a poet
who sang and read verse
one was a peasant
who drank and who cursed
before you decide
who's cruel and who's kind
let me explain
what i felt
in my heart and my mind

the artist was tender
but suffered from guilt
making him sorry
the following day
and he made me feel guilty
the very same way
in his bed on the following day
the other would take me
and feel no remorse
he'd wake with a smile
in the bed where we lay
and he made me smile
in the very same way
in his bed on the following day

the blow to my soul
by fear and taboos
cut deeper far
than a bodily bruise
and the one who was gentle
hurt me much more
than the one who was rough
and made love on the floor.

v/
witnesses to confusion

mary c. brown and
the hollywood sign

you know
the hollywood sign
that stands
in the hollywood hills
i don't think
the christ of the andes
ever blessed
so many ills

the hollywood sign
seems to smile
like it's

constantly saying cheese
i doubt if
the statue of liberty
ever welcomed
more refugees

give me your poor
your tired your pimps
your carhops
your cowboys
your midgets
your chimps
give me your freaks
give me your flunkies
your starlets
your whores
give me your junkies

mary cecilia brown
rode to town
on a malibu bus
she climbed to the top
of the hollywood sign
and with the
smallest possible fuss
she jumped off the letter "h"
'cause she did not
become a star

she died in less
than a minute and a half
she looked a bit like
hedy lamarr

sometimes
i have this dream
when the time comes
for me to go
i will hang myself
from the hollywood sign
from the second
or third letter "o"

when mary cecilia jumped
she finally made
the grade
her name was in
the obituary column
of both of the
daily trades

i hope
the hollywood sign
cries for the town
it touches
the lady of lourdes
in her grotto

saw fewer cripples
and crutches

give me your poor
your maladjusted
your sick and your beat
your sad
and your busted
give me your has-beens
give me your twisted
your loners
your losers
give me your black-listed

you know
the hollywood sign
witness
to our confusion
a symbol of dreams
turns out to be
a sign of disillusion.

the veterans' big parade

in the veterans' big parade
marched the businessmen's brigade
while behind the high school band
the ladies' fife and drum corps played
in the veterans' big parade
the flag flew high and free

down they marched to fourth and main
our soldiers died but not in vain
god was with us
that's for sure
he proved it 'cause
it didn't rain

balloons batons you wanted to cry
the best day in july

at the veterans' cemetery
then the services were said
there the mayor's first assistant
wiped his glasses
put them on
and read
ba ba ba ba ba
ba ba ba ba
we're gathered here
dear friends today
to show our brave boys
where they lay
we are with them all the way
and i think it's safe to say
they are not alone
they are not alone

all the widows proudly smiled
(except for one with an infant child)
picnic time was then announced
and all the little kids went wild
picnic blankets then were spread
and the beer flowed fast and free

there were clams and corn on the cob
to feed the celebrating mob

(once in a while
i don't know why
the infant child
began to sob)
other than that it was new year's eve
till it was time to leave

then a fine hawaiian band
played and sang
aloha oh
and their voices drifted low
between the crosses
painted white
row on row on row
ba ba ba ba ba
ba ba ba ba
aloha oh
and so good-bye
till next year boys
next july
we are with you
all the way
and i think
it's safe to say
you are not
alone
you are not
alone.

michael michael

michael michael
superman
muscle-bound
and supertan
leather jacket
denim pants
never did learn
how to dance
how to dance
digs karate
raps on zen
michael makes it

best with men
digs karate
raps on zen
michael makes it
best with men

michael michael
superman
muscle-bound
and supertan
when he walks
and talks
and moves
michael proves
and proves
and proves
michael is a
hyper superman

pushes acid
peddles hash
that's how michael
gets his stash
rides his cycle
like a king
knows his number
does his thing
does his thing

and if he wants to
he can con
any bird
he's turning on
if he wants to
he can con
any bird
he's turning on

michael michael
superman
muscle-bound
and supertan
when he walks
and talks
and moves
michael proves
and proves
and proves
michael is a
hyper superman

but
late at night
he sometimes seems
to hear
his mother's voice
in dreams

calling to him
clear and plain
but she calls him
mary jane
mary jane
and michael answers
plain and clear
i am coming
mother dear
michael answers
plain and clear
i am coming
mother dear

michael michael
superman
muscle-bound
and supertan
when he walks
and talks
and moves
michael proves
and proves
and proves
michael is a
hyper superman
a superman.

for sylvia
who killed herself
in 1963

i have been
where sylvia's been
she did not survive
i came back
from where she was
i'm still
half alive

i saw all
that sylvia saw
both our minds
were burned

100

she went closer
to the sun
she did not
return

sylvia soared
on wings of fear
i flew too
but not so far
sylvia strayed
sylvia stayed
too long
sylvia shaped
and sculpted poems
from the granite
of a star
all that i
could do was try
to carve a simple song

her light
was bright as
seraphim
my candle-wick
was dim
yet we both felt
our spirits melt

'neath sun
without a scrim

i envied sylvia
ariel eyed
and one of us
one of us
died.

VI /
listen and it all begins to fit

i can't go on

i can't go on
i mean
i can't go on
i really
can't go on
i swear
i can't go on

so
i guess
i'll get up
and go on.

scared to be alone

we never stop to wonder
till a person's gone
we never yearn
to know him
till he's traveled on
when someone is around us
we never stop to ask
hey what's behind your mirror
hey who's beneath your mask
we never stop to wonder
till a person's gone
we never yearn
to know him

till he's packed
and traveled on

sweet marilyn monroe
on the silver screen
platinum reflection
in a movie magazine
well did you ever
have a headache?
did your mama own a gramophone?
did you like to be an actress?
were you scared
to be alone?

we never stop to wonder
till a person's gone
we never yearn
to know him
till he's traveled on
when someone is around us
we don't know what we're seeing
we take a polaroid picture
to find the human being
we never stop to wonder
till a person's gone
we never yearn
to know him
till he's packed
and traveled on

sweet beautiful jesus
on a painted cross
polystyrene body
with a superficial gloss
hey were you
jealous of your father?
were you short
when you were fully grown?
did you like to walk on water?
were you scared
to be alone?

i think perhaps tomorrow
i'll try to make a friend
to really get
to know him
instead of pretend
i'll ask him if his feet hurt
has he burdens to be shared
and if he doesn't walk away
i'll ask him
if he's scared
and if he doesn't walk away
if his eyes don't
turn to stone
i'll ask him
if he's scared
to be alone.

mythical kings and iguanas

i have flown
to star-stained heights
on bent and battered wings
in search of
mythical kings
mythical kings
sure that everything of worth
is in the sky and not the earth
and i never learned
to make my way
down
down

down
where the iguanas play

i have ridden
comet tails
in search of magic rings
to conjure
mythical kings
mythical kings
singing scraps of angel-song
high is right and low is wrong
and i never taught
myself to give
down
down
down
where the iguanas live

astral walks i try to take
i sit and throw i ching
aesthetic bards
and tarot cards
are the cords
to which i cling
don't break my strings
(i wish you would)
or i will fall
(i wish i could

i wish i could
i wish i could)

curse the mind
that mounts the clouds
in search of mythical kings
and only
mystical things
mystical things
cry for the soul
that will not face
the body as an equal place
and i never learned
to touch for real
or feel the things
iguanas feel
down
down
down
where they play
teach me
teach me
teach me
reach me.

for r.d.l.

broken soul

(schiz: broken
phrenos: soul)

if i could take you love
on a voyage
from outer to inner
from a sort of life
to a kind of death
beyond heartbeat
beyond breath
beyond back
if i could take you there
(i have been you know)
would you come with me?
have you courage to go?

if i could lead you love
on a voyage
from here now
to no now
from the selfish time
to the timeless self
behind demons
behind beginnings
behind light
if i could take you there
oh the things you'd see
you may lose your way
of course
there is no guarantee

you will become entangled
in the simultaneous vision
of sea floors
and far stars
one eye pointed up and out
the other pointed down and in
and your
self
groping stunned and unbalanced
between the two
you will break your soul
be sure
broken soul

broken defenses
lose your mind
come to your senses

if i could take you love
then return you
from inner to inner/outer
from the eternal womb
through a second birth
into then now
with all you in you
split into one
if i could take you there
if you would explore
if i could tell you love
      there is more.

listen

i no longer plead with heaven
or go rummaging in books
for answers to the questions
life contains
now i listen
listen
listen to this inner thing resounding
in the pulsing and the pounding
of my infant ancient veins

i no longer seek instruction
from my father and my mother

i have mastered
all their pleasures and their pain
no i listen
listen
listen to this inner thing resounding
in the pulsing and the pounding
of my infant ancient veins

the feeling in my bloodflow
is a simple thing y'see
everything and nothing
in the parody is me
i'm the hero
i'm the villain
the beginning and the end
i'm creator
i'm destroyer
i'm the enemy the friend
i'm an animal
a spirit
flying high and falling down
i am special
i'm important
i am sacred
i'm a clown
so i stumble through the chaos
dragging clumsily behind me
all the eggshells
and the fish scales

and the fur pelts of my past
while this thing goes on
inside me at one with all
the vastness
the fantasies
and fictions
and when all the contradictions
come together
come together
they will fit

the feeling in my bloodflow
is a simple thing y'see
i am it
i am it
we are everything and nothing
but that's how to play the game
in these weather beaten bodies
with these god forsaken brains
we can listen
listen
listen to the universe resounding
in the pulsing and the pounding
of our infant ancient veins
listen
listen
listen and it all begins to fit
you are it
you are it